Wild Flowers

PAULA JOYCE

© THE MEDICI SOCIETY LTD
LONDON · 1995
Printed in England · ISBN 0 85503 061 5

GARDEN WEEDS

1 **Shepherd's Purse** *Capsella bursa-pastoris*. Cabbage Family. Ht: to 40 cm. Flowers throughout the year. Named from the shape of its seed pods which resemble purses carried by shepherds in the old days. It is also known in some parts of the country as Mother's Heart. It is very common.

2 **Black Medick** *Medicago lupulina*. Pea Family. Ht: to 50 cm trailing. Flowers April to August. A common plant of grassy places. The tiny seeds turn black when ripe.

3 **Ribwort Plantain** *Plantago lanceolata*. Plantain Family. Ht: to 50 cm. Flowers April to October. A tough plant with ribbed leaves. In a game called Soldiers, children strike one flower-head against another to see which breaks first.

4 **Ground Ivy** *Glechoma hederacea*. Mint Family. Ht: to 40 cm creeping. Flowers March to June. This plant, with its square stem, creeps along the ground. It is not related to Ivy.

5 **Groundsel** *Senecio vulgaris*. Daisy Family. Ht: to 40 cm. Flowers throughout the year. A widespread plant gathered to feed pet rabbits, and the seeds are fed to cage birds. When the fluffy seed-head is ripe, the individual seeds on their silken parachutes are blown away on the wind.

6 **Common Field Speedwell** *Veronica persica*. Snapdragon Family. Ht: to 35 cm sprawling. Flowers throughout the year. Of the many varieties this one can be recognised by its bright blue flowers with white lower petal.

7 **Daisy** *Bellis perennis*. Daisy Family. Ht: to 20 cm. Flowers all through the year. During bad weather, and when the sun sets, the flowers close—hence its name Day's Eye. Each flower-head is actually made up of many tiny flowers. Daisy chains are made by making a small slit at the bottom of a stalk and threading another stalk through—and so on.

8 **Dandelion** *Taraxacum officinale*. Daisy Family. Ht: to 40 cm. Flowers March to October. Its name is derived from the French Dent-de-lion (lion's teeth), referring to the jagged leaf edges. The flower only opens in the sun and is actually made up of many flower-heads. The fluffy seed head, called a 'clock', is used by children to tell the time—one puff for each hour, until all the fruits have been blown away.

9 **Lesser** or **Field Bindweed** *Convolvulus arvensis*. Bindweed Family. Ht: 150 cm creeping. Flowers June to September. The long stems twine round other plants as they trail along the ground and over low-lying shrubs.

10 **Stinging Nettle** *Urtica dioica*. Nettle family. Ht: to 150 cm. Flowers June to October. The stem and leaves are covered with tiny hairs which secrete a poison. When touched these hairs break, piercing the skin and causing it to itch and burn. Rubbing with a Dock leaf relieves the itch. Caterpillars of the Peacock and Red Admiral butterflies live on nettle leaves.

Dandelion 'clock'

1

2

3

5

4

6

7

8

9

10

HEDGEROW

1 Dog Rose *Rosa canina*. Rose Family. Ht: to 3 m. Flowers June to August. This lovely roadside plant has pink and white flowers which are sweetly scented and are followed in autumn by red hips. After the frost has softened them, these are eaten by the birds. Downward curving thorns help this plant to climb high up hedges and bushes. This is the earliest of the wild roses.

2 Wild Crab Apple *Malus sylvestris*. Rose Family. Ht: to 120 cm. Flowers April to May. This small, and sometimes thorny, tree bears white or pink blossom, followed by small green apples. Although sour to eat, the fruit makes good jelly. It is from this tree that all other apple trees have been cultivated.

Crab Apple blossom

3 Hazel *Corylus avellana*. Hazel Family. Ht: to 6 m. Flowers January to March. In February the fluffy male catkins scatter their pollen on the tiny female scarlet flowers. The nuts ripen in autumn and are good to eat. Some are stored away by squirrels for later in the winter when food is scarce.

4 Traveller's Joy *Clematis vitalba*. Buttercup Family. Ht: to 3 m rambling. Flowers July to August. The woody and often very thick stems of this plant curl tightly round anything they can, and so climb up and over trees and hedgerows. In autumn the fluffy white seed-heads form and stay throughout the winter until blown away by the wind. Hence its other name: Old Man's Beard.

Traveller's Joy seed-head

5 Woody Nightshade or **Bittersweet** *Solanum dulcamara*. Nightshade Family. Ht: to 2 m trailing. Flowers June to September. The poisonous berries which follow the purple flowers range in colour from green through to scarlet.

6 Blackberry or **Bramble** *Rubus fruticosus*. Rose Family. Ht: to 4.5 m trailing. Flowers May to September. This plant, whose long prickly stems clamber up and over hedges and bushes, has delicious berries. The flowers of the many species vary from white to pink.

7 Honeysuckle *Lonicera periclymenum*. Honeysuckle Family. Ht: 5.5 m climbing. Flowers June to September. The flowers are sweetly scented, particularly at night when they are visited by moths. The crimson berries are poisonous.

Dog Rose hip   Blackberry fruit   Woody Nightshade berries   Honeysuckle berries

2

3

5

6

7

PASTURES

1 Creeping Thistle *Cirsium arvense*. Daisy Family. Ht: to 130 cm. Flowers June to September. A common plant whose flowers attract butterflies and bees. The stem is smooth but the leaves are very prickly. The long creeping roots give it its name. In autumn the fluffy seeds form and when ripe are dispersed by the wind.

2 Cowslip *Primula veris*. Primrose Family. Ht: to 30 cm. Flowers April to June. This plant grows best out in the open on chalky hillsides. Once common, it has now become scarce through over-picking and so is protected. Orange spots on the petals act as guidelines for bees searching for nectar.

3 Perennial Rye Grass *Lolium perenne*. Grass Family. Ht: to 90 cm. Flowers May to August. Good winter food for cattle. This grass is also often sown on playing fields as it is very tough.

4 Ox-Eye Daisy or **Marguerite** *Chrysanthemum leucanthemum*. Daisy Family. Ht: to 70 cm. Flowers May to September. An old game is to pluck the petals one by one saying 'He loves me, he loves me not'. The flowers close at night and in bad weather.

5 Meadow or **Field Buttercup** *Ranunculus acris*. Buttercup Family. Ht: to 80 cm. Flowers May to September. A field of golden buttercups is a lovely sight, but care should be taken as they are poisonous and held too long can burn the skin. If the flower is held under the chin and the skin glows yellow, it is said the person likes butter.

6 Timothy Grass *Phleum pratense*. Grass Family. Ht: to 130 cm. Flowers June to August. Another name is Cat's Tail Grass because of the furry look of the plump flower-head. This grass is grown as food for cattle.

7 Red Clover *Trifolium pratense*. Pea Family. Ht: to 40 cm. Flowers May to September. Grown as fodder for cows and sheep. Clover honey is made from the nectar collected by bees from the sweet smelling flowers.

8 Cocksfoot Grass *Dactylis glomerata*. Grass Family. Ht: to 105 cm. Flowers June to September. A fodder plant common throughout the countryside.

9 White or **Dutch Clover** *Trifolium repens*. Pea Family. Ht: to 40 cm. Flowers May to September. This plant was brought over from Holland as a food crop for cows and sheep. Like the Red Clover, its nectar attracts bees. Most clover leaves have three sections, but the rare 4-leaved clover is said to bring the finder good luck.

10 Birdsfoot-Trefoil *Lotus corniculatus*. Pea Family. Ht: to 40 cm. Flowers May to September. This plant has over 70 local names, including Lady's Slipper and Bacon & Eggs, but the most common is Birdsfoot-Trefoil, so called because when ripe its seed pods look like a bird's claw. This is the food plant of the caterpillar of the Common Blue Butterfly.

Birdsfoot-Trefoil seed pod

WATER MEADOWS and RIVERSIDES

1 Great Reed-Mace *Typha latifolia*. Reed-Mace Family. Ht: 2–5 m. Flowers June to July. When young, the tall pokers which grow on the banks of rivers and lakes are green, but they darken to brown throughout the summer. The following March the pokers burst open, allowing the hundreds of seeds to be blown away by the wind.

2 Ragged Robin *Lychnis flos-cuculi*. Pink Family. Ht: to 70 cm. Flowers May to July. Found in wet meadows, this plant gets its Latin name, *flos-cuculi*, meaning flower of the cuckoo, from the time of year it is in bloom. Attracted by the scent, moths visit the flowers in the evening.

3 Marsh Marigold or **Kingcup** *Caltha palustris*. Buttercup Family. Ht: to 40 cm. Flowers March to April. This handsome plant can be found in marshy water meadows in early spring.

4 Great Hairy Willowherb *Epilobium hirsutum*. Willowherb Family. Ht: 150 cm. Flowers June to August. Commonly found in damp ditches and by riversides, this plant has a hairy stem and leaf back. In autumn the long seed pods form and when ripe burst open and the silky seeds are blown away on the wind. Another name is Codlins & Cream.

5 Yellow Iris or **Flag** *Iris pseudacorus*. Iris Family. Ht: 100 cm. Flowers May to August. This plant likes to grow at the water's edge. Each stem has 2 to 3 flowers which bloom one at a time. After the flowers, the seed pods form and when ripe split open. The seeds then fall into the water and float away.

6 Meadowsweet *Filipendula ulmaria*. Rose Family. Ht: 120 cm. Flowers June to September. Before carpets, this plant was spread on the floor amongst the rushes because of its sweet smell. Also known as Queen of the Meadows.

7 Water Forget-Me-Not *Myosotis scorpioides*. Borage Family. Ht: to 40 cm. Flowers May to September. This plant, whose flowers range from blue to pink and mauve, usually grows in shallow streams and ditches. It has larger flowers and thicker stems than other Forget-Me-Nots.

8 Lady's Smock *Cardamine pratensis*. Cabbage Family. Ht: to 40 cm. Flowers May to September. Found growing in water meadows, the leaves are the favourite food of the Orange-tipped Butterfly. The flowers vary in colour from pink to lilac and white. Also called Cuckoo Flower because it is thought to bloom when the first cuckoo is heard in springtime.

Orange-tipped Butterfly on Lady's Smock

ARABLE FIELDS

1 Red Deadnettle *Lamium purpureum*. Mint Family. Ht: to 35 cm. Flowers March to November. This nettle does not sting. The downy leaves often have a reddish tinge and give off a pungent smell when crushed. Its stems are square.

2 Charlock or **Wild Mustard** *Sinapis arvensis*. Cabbage Family. Ht: to 70 cm. Flowers April to September. Often to be seen in fields of corn, this tall plant is not popular with farmers who kill it with weedkiller.

3 Scentless Mayweed *Matricaria maritima*. Daisy Family. Ht: to 55 cm. Flowers May to September. Farmers dislike all the different Mayweeds. Even weedkiller does not succeed in getting rid of them.

4 Common Field Poppy *Papaver rhoeas*. Poppy Family. Ht: to 50 cm. Flowers June to September. Sometimes whole fields of scarlet poppies can be seen, although this is rare. In the bud the petals are crushed tightly together, but all the creases fall out as the flower opens. The seed-head is like a tiny pepper-pot which nods to and fro in the wind, scattering hundreds of tiny seeds.

Poppy seed-head

5 Wild Pansy or **Heartsease** *Viola tricolor*. Violet Family. Ht: to 30 cm. Flowers April to September. Found in cornfields, the colour of the flowers varies, but usually they are cream with purple or blue upper petals. When the seed case is ripe it bursts open and the seeds shoot out.

Wild Pansy seed-head

6 Germander Speedwell *Veronica chamaedrys*. Snapdragon Family. Ht: to 30 cm. Flowers March to July. The most common of all the Speedwells, this plant grows alongside fields and roads; hence 'Speed you well' on your journey. It has hairs in two rows up its stem.

7 Scarlet Pimpernel *Anagallis arvensis*. Primrose Family. Ht: to 18 cm. Flowers May to September. Although the flowers are usually red they can also be pink, white or blue. As this flower does not open in cold weather and closes before it is going to rain, another name for it is Poor Man's Weather-glass.

Scarlet Pimpernel seed-head

8 Common Fumitory *Fumaria officinalis*. Fumitory Family. Ht: to 40 cm creeping. Flowers May to October. It is said that when this plant is pulled out of the ground it gives off a smoky smell, hence its Latin name which means Smoke of the Earth.

SHADY AND WASTE PLACES,
roadsides and disused railway cuttings

1 Greater Knapweed *Centaurea scabiosa*. Daisy Family. Ht: to 70 cm. Flowers June to September. Found on roadsides, this plant is more common on chalky soils in the south than in the rest of the country. There is a rare version which has white flowers.

2 Rosebay Willowherb or **Fireweed** *Epilobium angustifolium*. Willowherb Family. Ht: 140 cm. Flowers July to September. Once rare, this plant has now spread everywhere and the tall flower spikes can be seen along roadsides, on building sites and banks. When the seed pods ripen in autumn they burst open and the thousands of fleecy seeds are spread by the wind.

3 Common Toadflax *Linaria vulgaris*. Snapdragon Family. Ht: to 60 cm. Flowers June to September. Common along railway banks. The flowers, sometimes called Bunny Rabbits, attract bees.

4 Meadow Cranesbill *Geranium pratense*. Geranium Family. Ht: to 70 cm. Flowers May to September. The shape of the fruit of this plant resembles the bill of a Crane, hence its name. Found on roadsides in the south, its leaves turn red in autumn.

5 Self Heal *Prunella vulgaris*. Mint Family. Ht: to 25 cm creeping. Flowers June to September. This creeping plant of waste places and roadsides has hairy leaves and a square stem. It was once thought to help wounds to heal quickly. When the seeds are ripe they are dispersed by falling raindrops.

Rosebay Willowherb seed-head

6 Lady's Bedstraw *Galium verum*. Bedstraw Family. Ht: to 70 cm. Flowers June to August. A square-stemmed plant whose flowers give off a sweet smell of honey in the evenings.

7 Yarrow *Achillea millefolium*. Daisy Family. Ht: to 55 cm. Flowers May to October. This strong stemmed plant carries flowers which can vary from white to pink or mauve. Its other name, Milfoil, means thousands of leaves.

8 Wild Strawberry *Fragaria vesca*. Rose Family. Ht: to 30 cm. Flowers April to July. Commonly found along disused railway tracks and the borders of woods. This plant spreads by sending out runners to form new plants. The small fruits are delicious to eat and it is the tiny pips on the surface which are the seeds.

1

2

3

4

5

6

7

8

WOODLAND

1 Foxglove *Digitalis purpurea.* Snapdragon Family. Ht: 150 cm. Flowers June to September. Found in open glades, this flower is also called Fairies' Thimbles. The spots inside guide the bees to the nectar. Although the drug Digitalis extracted from its leaves is very valuable in the treatment of heart disease, this is a very poisonous plant.

2 Primrose *Primula vulgaris.* Primrose Family. Ht: to 20 cm. Flowers February to May. This lovely flower derives its name from Prima Rosa— the 'first rose' of spring. There are two types: Pin-eyed and Thrum-eyed. Insects carry pollen from one type to another, ensuring cross-pollination.

Pin-eyed Primrose   Thrum-eyed Primrose

3 Wood Anemone *Anemone nemorosa.* Buttercup Family. Ht: to 20 cm. Flowers March to April. These delicate flowers, which nod in the breeze on their slender stems, are commonly called Wind-flowers.

4 Bluebell *Endymion non-scriptus.* Lily Family. Ht: to 50 cm. Flowers May to June. In springtime these lovely wild hyacinths carpet the woods, particularly of oak. Bluebells have contractile roots— as new bulbs form on top of the soil, they are drawn down into the earth by the tap root.

5 Ivy *Hedera helix.* Ivy Family. Ht: to 25 m. Flowers September to November. This evergreen plant creeps along the ground and climbs over walls and trees. The upper stems have a different-shaped leaf and, late in the year, bear flowers and fruit, welcome food for the birds in winter.

Ivy leaf

6 Common Dog Violet *Viola riviniana.* Violet Family. Ht: to 25 cm. Flowers April to June. The scentless flowers of this violet can be distinguished from other varieties by their square-shaped faces. When ripe the seed pods burst open and the seeds are propelled out to be scattered by the wind.

7 Lords & Ladies or **Wild Arum** *Arum maculatum.* Arum Family. Ht: to 45 cm. Flowers April to June. By its smell this strange flower attracts flies which become trapped at the bottom of the spathe. Later, when the flower dies the flies escape and when visiting the next Arum transfer pollen to it. The berries, which develop in July, are very poisonous. The leaves are sometimes spotted.

Inside base of an Arum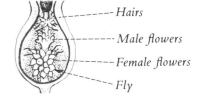

Hairs
Male flowers
Female flowers
Fly

8 Lesser Celandine *Ranunculus ficaria.* Buttercup Family. Ht: to 20 cm. Flowers March to May. This lovely but poisonous plant is one of the first to flower in the spring. The number of glossy, gold petals of each flower varies between 8 and 12, and they open and close with the sun.

1

2

3

4

5

6

7

8

FRESH WATER

1   Branched Bur-Reed *Sparganium erectum*. Bur-Reed Family. Ht: 150 cm. Flowers June to August. Grows in shallow water alongside rivers and ditches. Each plant carries both male and female flowers.

2   Water Plantain *Alisma plantago-aquatica*. Water Plantain Family. Ht: to 100 cm. Flowers June to August. This tall plant which is found at the side of ponds, lakes, and rivers has very tiny 3-petalled flowers.

3   Arrow Head *Sagittaria sagittifolia*. Water Plantain Family. Ht: to 90 cm. Flowers June to August. It is the tall, arrow-shaped leaves, carried above the water on 3-sided stalks, that give this plant its name. Its other leaves, floating on the water and submerged beneath, are differently shaped.

4   Brooklime *Veronica beccabunga*. Snapdragon Family. Ht: to 60 cm. Flowers May to August. This plant is found in muddy and wet places.

5   Yellow Water-Lily *Nuphar lutea*. Water-Lily Family. Floating. Flowers June to August. This plant has its roots in the mud at the bottom of ponds or rivers. The leaves float on the surface, but the flowers stand up out of it.

6   Amphibious or **Water Bistort** *Polygonum amphibium*. Dock Family. Floating. Flowers July to September. The flower-heads of this plant stand upright from the surface of slow moving rivers and pools.

7   White Water-Lily *Nymphaea alba*. Water-Lily Family. Floating. Flowers July to August. Rooting in the mud of still pools and lakes, the leaves and large beautiful flowers of this plant float on the surface. When the seed pod ripens and bursts, the seeds float away.

White Water-Lily plant

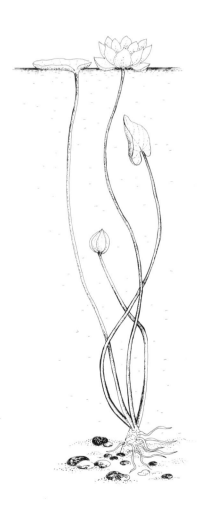

SEA SHORE and salt marshes

1 Yellow Horned Poppy *Glaucium flavum*. Poppy Family. Ht: to 75 cm. Flowers June to September. Found on the shingle, this plant gets its name from its seed pods which can grow as long as 20 cm. Each flower lasts for just a day.

2 Sea Lavender *Limonium vulgare*. Sea Lavender Family. Ht: to 30 cm. Flowers July to October. Salt marshes are found carpeted with these mauve flowers which attract bees.

3 Sea Bindweed *Calystegia soldanella*. Bindweed Family. Ht: to 50 cm creeping. Flowers June to August. The stems of this plant creep along the shoreline. The flowers are similar but smaller than the white Bindweed which trails over the hedgerows. Its leaves are kidney shaped.

4 Thrift *Armeria maritima*. Sea Lavender Family. Ht: to 20 cm. Flowers April to August. Also called Sea Pink and Lady's Pincushion, this plant is found on cliffs and salt marshes. The pink or white flowers grow out of cushions of grass-like leaves. Sometimes a whole cliff-side appears pink with these pretty flowers.

5 Yellow Biting Stonecrop *Sedum acre*. Stonecrop Family. Ht: to 10 cm. Flowers May to July. Also called Wallpepper. Grows on walls and sandhills as well as shingle beaches.

6 Sea Campion *Silene maritima*. Pink Family. Ht: to 25 cm. Flowers June to August. Growing mainly on shingle, this plant differs from Bladder Campion in that it has broader petals and not all its shoots bear flowers.

7 Golden Samphire *Inula crithmoides*. Daisy Family. Ht: to 80 cm. Flowers July to October. This fleshy-leaved plant is found on shingle and salt marshes, but is quite rare.

8 Sea Aster *Aster tripolium*. Daisy Family. Ht: to 50 cm. Flowers July to October. The name Aster means Star. This wild Michaelmas Daisy is found on muddy salt marshes. Like many plants of the sea shore, the thick leaves and stem store water.

Cushion of Sea Pinks

1

2

3

4

5

6

7

8

MOORLAND AND HEATHS

1 Heather or **Ling** *Calluna vulgaris*. Heath Family. Ht: to 80 cm. Flowers July to September. This very common evergreen heather, which grows in large clumps, is used as a fuel, and also to feed sheep. Delicious heather honey is produced by bees from the nectar of its flowers.

2 Gorse, Whin or **Furze** *Ulex europaeus*. Pea Family. Ht: to 2 m. Flowers throughout the year. This prickly shrub grows in dense masses, often covering wide areas. The seed pods can be heard popping open when ripe. There is an old saying 'When gorse is out of bloom, kissing is out of season'.

Gorse pods

3 Harebell or **Scottish Bluebell** *Campanula rotundifolia*. Bellflower Family. Ht: to 45 cm. Flowers July to September. This delicate scentless flower is widespread in dry grassy places.

4 Bell Heather *Erica cinerea*. Heath Family. Ht: to 55 cm. Flowers May to September. Butterflies and bumblebees visit the sweet-smelling flowers. Grows in large clumps on the moors.

5 Eye Bright *Euphrasia officinalis* (agg.). Snapdragon Family. Ht: to 25 cm. Flowers June to October. The many species of this plant are hard to tell apart. Its name comes from an extract once used to brighten eyes.

6 Tormentil *Potentilla erecta*. Rose Family. Ht: to 25 cm creeping. Flowers May to September. Found on heaths throughout Britain, the roots of this plant were formerly used in the treatment of stomach ailments.

7 Cross-Leaved or **Bog Heath** *Erica tetralix*. Heath Family. Ht: to 40 cm. Flowers June to September. Common on bogs and moist places, the flowers of this plant vary from white to rose, and are much visited by bees. Like the other heathers, this also grows in large clumps.

8 Bilberry, Blaeberry or **Whortleberry** *Vaccinium myrtillus*. Heath Family. Ht: to 50 cm. Flowers April to June. This plant is found on moors and mountains. The fruit is good to eat.

9 Bracken (Fern) *Pteridium aquilinum*. Fern Family. Ht: 130 cm. Spores ripen from July to August. The colour illustration shows only a frond of this most common fern. When first it pierces the surface of the earth it looks like a tiny shepherd's crook. In autumn the fronds turn to gold and amber.

CHALK DOWNS

1 Spindle *Euonymus europaeus*. Spindle Family. Ht: to 6 m. Flowers May to June. Berries of this shrub (which are poisonous) are a lovely sight in autumn with the orange seeds bursting out from the pink cases. A very hard wood, once used to make spindles—hence its name—and also skewers. The flowers are small, 4-petalled, and green.

2 Common Rock-Rose *Helianthemum nummularium*. Rock-Rose Family. Ht: to 30 cm. Flowers May to September. The flowers of this trailing plant vary from white to creamy yellow or orange in colour. The underneath of the leaves is covered with white hairs.

3 Quaking Grass *Briza media*. Grass Family. Ht: to 90 cm. Flowers June to August. This attractive grass gets its name from the way it shivers in the wind.

4 Pyramidal Orchid *Anacamptis pyramidalis*. Orchid Family. Ht: to 45 cm. Flowers June to August. This orchid, with its flowers arranged in a pyramid shape, attracts butterflies and moths.

5 Horseshoe Vetch *Hippocrepis comosa*. Pea Family. Ht: to 30 cm. Flowers May to July. This is the food plant for the caterpillars of the Chalk Hill Blue Butterfly. The horseshoe-shaped parts of the seed pod give it its name.

6 Wild Carrot *Daucus carota*. Carrot Family. Ht: to 90 cm. Flowers June to August. Widespread in grassy places. Every flower-head carries a red or purple flower in the middle, which attracts insects.

7 Devil's Bit Scabious *Succisa pratensis*. Teasel Family. Ht: to 80 cm. Flowers June to October. Found also in damp grassy places, the root of this plant is said to have been bitten off by the Devil, hence its name. The flowers are sometimes pink.

8 Bee Orchid *Ophrys apifera*. Orchid Family. Ht: to 45 cm. Flowers June and July. As its name implies, this flower looks very like a resting bee. This encourages real bees to visit it. In this way pollen is carried from flower to flower.

9 Common Milkwort *Polygala vulgaris*. Milkwort Family. Ht: to 20 cm. Flowers May to September. The flowers of this plant can be blue, pink or white.

Wild Carrot—seed head showing how the shape of the flower head alters as the seeds form.

1

2

3

4

5

6

7

8

9

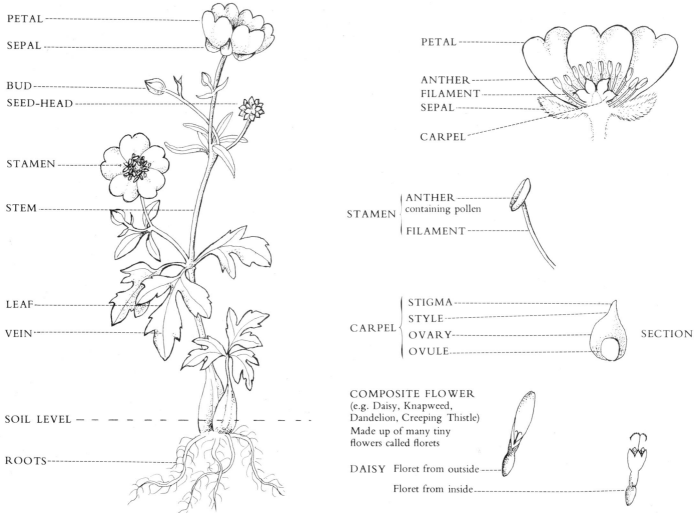

PARTS OF A PLANT
(BUTTERCUP)

PETAL
SEPAL
BUD
SEED-HEAD
STAMEN
STEM
LEAF
VEIN
SOIL LEVEL
ROOTS

BUTTERCUP FLOWER LONGITUDINALLY
CUT ACROSS MIDDLE

PETAL
ANTHER
FILAMENT
SEPAL
CARPEL

STAMEN { ANTHER
containing pollen
FILAMENT }

CARPEL { STIGMA
STYLE
OVARY
OVULE }   SECTION

COMPOSITE FLOWER
(e.g. Daisy, Knapweed,
Dandelion, Creeping Thistle)
Made up of many tiny
flowers called florets

DAISY Floret from outside
Floret from inside

Every part of a plant has an important role to play in helping to ensure that its species
continues to reproduce. An understanding of the functions of each part increases the
interest in the study of wild flowers. Many books have been published on the subject for
those who want to know more.